The effects of parents' employment on children's lives

John Ermisch and Marco Francesconi

Published for the Joseph Rowntree Foundation by the
Family Policy Studies Centre
9 Tavistock Place, London WC1H 9SN
Tel: +44 (0)20 7388 5900

ISBN 1 901455 60 2

March 2001

British Library Catalogue-in-Publication Data
A catalogue record for this book is available from the British
Library.

The **Family Policy Studies Centre** is an independent body which
analyses family trends and the impact of policy. It is a centre of
research and information. The Centre's Governing Council
represents a wide spectrum of political opinion, as well as
professional, academic, faith, local authority and other interests.
The facts presented and views expressed in this report are those of
the author and not necessarily those of the Centre.

The **Joseph Rowntree Foundation** has supported this project as
part of its programme of research and innovative development
projects, which it hopes will be of value to policy-makers,
practitioners and service users. The facts presented and views
expressed in this report, however, are those of the authors and not
necessarily those of the Foundation.

Design and print by Intertype

Contents

1   **Introduction**   *7*

2   **The research design**   *10*

3   **The sample: young people and their families**   *13*

4   **The effects of parents' employment**   *25*

5   **Other influences**   *35*

6   **Conclusions**   *42*

References   *46*

Endnotes   *47*

Tables and figures

Table 3.1   The four samples *15*

Table 3.2   Average values of parents' employment variables *16*

Table 3.3   Mothers' employment patterns, by occupation and by their children's development stage *18*

Table 3.4   Parents' educational qualifications *20*

Table 3.5   Average measures of occupational status using the Hope-Goldthorpe index *20*

Table 3.6   Family structure *21*

Table 3.7   Outcomes among young people *22*

Table 4.1   Effects of an additional year of childhood maternal part-time and full-time employment on the probability of achieving A-level or more, by developmental stage *26*

Figure 3.1   Mothers' employment by child's development stage *17*

Figure 3.2   Percentage of mothers employed sometime during development stage *19*

Figure 4.1   Effects of an additional year of childhood maternal part-time and full-time employment on the probability of achieving A-level or more, by developmental stage *27*

Figure 4.2   Effects of an additional year of childhood maternal part-time and full-time employment on the probability of the child's economic inactivity, by developmental stage *29*

Figure 4.3   Effects of childhood maternal part-time and full-time employment on the probability of a high level of the child's psychological distress, by developmental stage *31*

Figure 4.4   Effects of an additional year of childhood maternal part-time and full-time employment on the annual probability of early childbearing, by developmental stage *32*

Figure 5.1   Effects of being female and being born one year later on outcomes *35*

Figure 5.2   Effects of age on outcomes *36*

Figure 5.3   Effects of mother's education level on outcomes *37*

Figure 5.4   Effects of father's education level on outcomes *37*

Figure 5.5   Effects of one unit higher Hope-Goldthorpe score on outcomes *38*

Figure 5.6   Effects of an additional sibling on outcomes *39*

Figure 5.7   Effects of being in a single-parent family on outcomes, by age at start *40*

Figure 5.8   Effects of being in a stepfamily on outcomes, by age at start *40*

About the authors

John Ermish is a Professor of Economics at the University of Essex and Fellow of the British Academy.

Marco Francesconi is a Senior Research Fellow at the Institute for Social and Economic Research at the University of Essex.

Institute for Social and Economic Research
University of Essex
Colchester CO 3SQ
United Kingdom

1 | Introduction

Parents play an important role in shaping the adult lives of their children. The way they use their time and money while children are growing up can have long-lasting consequences. In particular, the paid work done by fathers and mothers affects both the amount of income coming into the family and the time they have available to spend with their children. The longer-term effects that parents' employment patterns may have on children are relevant to many areas of public policy. The more so, since recent government initiatives have been designed to reduce dependency on state benefits and improve family finances by encouraging more parents to take up paid work – especially mothers and lone parents.

The aim of this research was to study the links between parents' employment patterns when their children were growing up and what happened in those children's lives – outcomes – when they became young adults. The study focuses on a number of outcomes, notably:

- educational attainment;
- employment and economic inactivity;
- mental health;

and, for women:

- childbearing at an early age.

An attempt to measure these connections had to take account of the ways other than employment patterns that families might influence children's long-term development. For that reason, the study also considered how far outcomes had been affected by other factors, notably:

- parents' own level of educational attainment;
- the number of siblings in a family;
- children's experiences of life in a lone-parent family;
- children's experiences of life in a stepfamily.

Research background

Mothers' employment

Previous research has yielded little consensus about the association between mothers' employment and outcomes for their children in young adulthood. Evidence from the United States, where most of the studies have been conducted, is mixed. Some researchers identify a significant adverse effect on children's educational achievement, while others find no significant effect, or even suggest a favourable impact (Haveman and Wolfe, 1995). Kathleen Kiernan's (1996) analysis of longitudinal data for British children born in 1958 found that having a mother in work when the child was aged 16 was associated with a higher probability of young women gaining qualifications. This was especially true of those from lone-parent families. However, there was no similar association that was statistically significant for young men. Another finding was that young women from lone-parent families whose mothers had been employed when their daughters were aged 16 were less likely to have become teenage mothers. There was no similar findings that reached statistical significance for young women whose families had remained intact. A study of working-class families living in East London used qualitative, case-study data on 550 children to suggest that children growing up in dual-earner families where the mothers were employed part-time tended to do better than others in terms of educational achievement (O'Brien and Jones, 1999).

The lack of agreement about the effects of mothers' paid employment on their children's subsequent achievements may partly reflect differences in the ways that studies have sought to take account of other relevant influences by applying statistical controls to their data. The need for controls is indisputable, since any correlation – whether positive or negative – is likely to reflect the impact of other factors on both the mothers' employment patterns and on parent–child relationships. However, the methods by which controls can be applied are necessarily complex and the scope for eliminating extraneous influences may be limited by the type of data available. This issue receives further discussion below when the methodology for the present study is described.

Fathers' employment

The long-term influence of fathers' employment on their children's lives is usually considered to occur through their contribution to family income. Few studies have concentrated on the influence that different patterns of work by fathers might exert during childhood. However, a small but growing literature in developmental psychology has examined the effects of early paternal employment on child development, with mixed results. In one American study, fathers' time in paid work was found to affect the amount, but not the quality, of interaction with infants (McHale and Huston, 1984). Another found that children whose fathers worked fewer hours during their first years of life exhibited more behavioural problems subsequently (Parcel and Menaghan, 1994). More recently it has been suggested that children's cognitive outcomes are poorer when their mothers work and their fathers do not during in the first year of life (Han, Waldfogel and Brooks-Gunn, 1999). However, a review of US studies (Harvey, 1999) concluded that

there were few significant effects on children's development that could be attributed to fathers' hours of employment.

Family structure

One important factor to take into account when studying the impact of parental employment is the type of family in which children have been raised. When a child's parents separate, or a child is born to parents who do not live together, the non-resident parent (usually the father) tends to spend less money on his children (Weiss and Willis, 1985). This lower expenditure is likely to be associated with children's lower educational attainment and subsequent difficulties in the labour market. By limiting labour market opportunities, lower spending by non-resident parents may also increase the chances of young women becoming mothers at an early age. In addition, family structure is likely to affect the amount of time that parents have available to spend with their children. This not only applies to non-resident parents, but also to resident parents who may be urged by the break up of the partnership to change their working arrangements. For example, some lone mothers may feel they must spend more time at home with their children, while others come under economic pressure to increase their hours of work (McLanahan and Sandefur, 1994).

There is rather more consensus among researchers on the association between children's experiences of life in a lone-parent family and their outcomes as young adults. In many American studies, it tends to be associated with lower educational attainment and a higher risk of early childbearing and giving birth outside marriage (see Haveman and Wolfe, 1995, for an overview). Kiernan

(1997), using UK longitudinal data, found that divorce during childhood was correlated with outcomes for educational attainment, economic situation, partnership formation, relationship breakdown and parenthood behaviour in adulthood, which were generally 'worse' than those for children from intact families. Her work builds on earlier work using samples from the National Child Development Study (NCDS) of British children born in 1958 (Ní Bhrolcháin, Chappel and Diamond,1994; Kiernan,1992; Cherlin, Kiernan and Chase-Lansdale,1995). All these studies have varied in the range and type of adjustments applied to the data to control for other family background and individual characteristics. However, a forthcoming study by Ermisch and Francesconi (2001b) uses a sample from the British Household Panel Study (BHPS) to reach a comparable conclusion: namely, that young people who have spent part of their childhood in a lone-parent family tend to achieve lower educational qualifications than those whose families remain intact. This is especially the case if they have experienced life in a lone-parent family before their sixth birthday.

2 | The research design

This research uses the British Household Panel Study (BHPS) to examine the impact of parents' employment patterns and childhood family structure on outcomes during young adulthood. The BHPS data set has the following advantages over that from the National Child Development Study (NCDS) and other birth cohort studies:

- The data are more recent and a better reflection of contemporary family life. The households tracked by BHPS have been interviewed annually since 1991, and the young adults who are the focus of this study were all born between 1970 and 1981. Mothers' employment and lone parenthood (to mention two salient changes) were much more common among BHPS families than when the 1958 NCDS cohort was growing up.
- Although the NCDS and 1970 British Cohort Study (BCS) have larger sample sizes and include more measures of non-economic background factors and children's early achievements, the BHPS yields more detailed information on parents' employment patterns. It is possible to measure parents' employment throughout their children's upbringing, rather than at a particular point in time.[1]
- Because the BHPS follows whole households, including siblings, it is possible to control the data for any unobserved influences in family background influences that are shared by children from the same family.[2]

Previous studies have tried to identify the impact of mothers' employment by interviewing a cross-section of young adults and obtaining retrospective information about their mother's working patterns when they were younger. As explained in the next chapter, there are real difficulties in attributing any 'cause and effect' relationship to associations identified this way. Our ability, using unique characteristics of the BHPS data, to compare outcomes for siblings with their parents' employment histories is more likely to identify any cause and effect relationships where they exist.

Choosing measurements

Working time

Ideally, a study of this kind would want to include measures of how much time parents spent with their children at different ages, and how much money they spent on them. But while there have been studies measuring the former, none have related that information to outcomes when children became adults. In the absence of 'time use' data, the next-best option – as with this study – is to measure the time that parents spent in paid employment. This allows us to establish how much time each parent had available outside work, but it also means we cannot be sure how that time was divided between interaction with their children and other activities. Some parents may have managed to boost their incomes by working more hours, but without reducing the time they spend with their children. It should also be borne in mind that parents' working hours can influence children in less quantifiable ways than family income: for example, the extent to which children value their parents' job status and view them as role models. Thus, even if the data suggested that parents spending less time with children tended to have adverse effects, there could be balancing factors related to the extra family income and other positive influences resulting from parents' spending more time at work.

Personal endowments

Another problem that arises when trying to measure the effects of parental employment is that parents make decisions about their working hours alongside other choices about the way their time and money are spent. It is especially important to remember that children are born into the world with personal attributes and individual abilities. These personal 'endowments', which include characteristics such as temperament and cognitive abilities, are genetically and culturally linked to their parents' own set of endowments. Moreover, parents are aware of these endowments, even when researchers are not. They take them into account when making decisions about how much time and money to devote to their children. For example, they may choose to spend more time with a child who has learning disabilities or encounters difficulties in school. Decisions about how much time and money they invest in their children's education will also be influenced by personal endowments. Parents who are highly-motivated and educated themselves will tend to put a high value on educating their own children.

It follows that any research attempt to reach an unbiased estimate of the links between parents' employment patterns and their children's educational attainments (and other outcomes) must account for the tendency for children with high endowments to gain better qualifications and to have parents whose own endowments are high. Highly-educated and motivated mothers may spend more of their time in employment and earn more money to spend on their children; but they may also spend more of their remaining time engaging their children in educational pursuits. There is, therefore, a distinct possibility that research showing a positive connection between mothers' working hours and their children's educational achievements might simply reflect a correlation between child's and parents' endowments. If so, it would be quite misleading to draw any general conclusion that mothers were increasing their children's chances of educational success by spending more time at work.

Using sibling differences as a control

These caveats underline the importance of controlling survey data on parental employment for other factors such as parents' educational attainment that affect their children's achievements. Yet it is also clear that no matter how many parental variables are measured and controlled for in a data set, they are still liable to omit some aspects of family background and parents' preferences that are correlated with their own and their children's endowments. However, the fact that parental endowments will usually be the same for *all* the children in a family, suggests a way in which a data set with information on siblings can be used to control for their influence. Thus, the information on brothers and sisters in the BHPS makes it possible to relate differences between the adult outcomes for siblings to differences in their mother's employment patterns at the time they were children. It is possible that a mother's employment pattern could be a response to idiosyncratic endowments among her children, such as giving birth to a mathematical genius. It is also possible that some children will experience a change in their parents' circumstances that never applied to their brothers or sisters – for example, a father developing an alcohol problem that not only damages their education, but also leads to their mother working longer hours. Even so, the data on sibling differences gathered by the BHPS delivers a valuable and unusual opportunity to control the data for parental endowments, increasing the likelihood that any association found between parents' employment during childhood and children's longer-term outcomes reflects a causal relationship.

For the reasons described above, studies which rely on comparisons *between* families to measure the associations between parents' employment and outcomes of their children do not provide a reliable estimate of the causal impact of parents' employment patterns. Even so, this report deliberately includes a series of these **between family estimates** calculated on a similar basis so that comparisons with the results of previous studies can be made. However, the **sibling difference estimates** based on comparisons *within* families control more reliably and comprehensively for family background, making it less likely that the results have been contaminated by unmeasured factors.

3 | The sample: young people and their families

The data analysed for this research come from a special sample selected using the first seven annual waves of the British Household Panel Study (BHPS). In Autumn 1991, the BHPS interviewed a representative sample of 5,500 households, containing about 10,000 people. The same individuals have been re-interviewed each successive year (the 'panel element'). However, if they leave their original households to form new households, then all the adult members of the new households are also interviewed as part of the study. Children in the original households are also interviewed once they reach the age of 16. Some 88 per cent of the original BHPS sample were re-interviewed for the second wave and the response rates from the third wave onwards have been consistently higher than 95 per cent. The BHPS data are, therefore, unlikely to suffer from any serious bias resulting from attrition. This means that the sample remained broadly representative of the population of Britain as it changed during the 1990s.

Sampling strategy

To estimate the effects of parents' paid work on their children's outcomes as young adults, we first matched young adults in the study to one or both of their biological parents interviewed in at least one of the seven years. We then used the information that parents had provided about their family and work backgrounds to determine the patterns of family structure and parental employment that applied when their children were growing up.

Family structure

The second wave (1992) of the BHPS gathered retrospective information on complete fertility, marital and cohabitation histories for all the adult panel members interviewed that year. This information was the basis of our understanding of whether the young adults in our sample had spent any time in a lone-parent family during the first 16 years of their childhood. For the purpose of analysis, children were defined as:

- being raised in an *intact* family if they had lived continuously with both biological parents, or with one biological and one adoptive parent;
- having spent time in a *lone-parent* family if they had ever lived with a biological or adoptive mother who was neither cohabiting nor married. This could happen if their parents had separated or divorced, or because they were born outside a live-in relationship and their mothers did not cohabit or marry within a year of the birth.[3] The ages at which children became part of a lone-parent family were divided into developmental stages (see below);[4]
- having lived in a *stepfamily* if they lived with a biological or adoptive mother who was cohabiting with, or married to, a person other than their biological fathers. As with membership of a lone-parent family, information was obtained about the developmental stages at which children became part of a stepfamily.

In addition, by matching young adults with their parents, we were able to measure other background characteristics such as the parents' ages at the time of the young person's birth, parents' educational backgrounds, and the number of brothers and sisters in each family.

Employment histories

The third wave (1993) of the BHPS gathered retrospective employment histories for each adult panel member interviewed that year. This included information about all the jobs they had held between the time they left full-time education and September 1990, when the BHPS began.

- Measurements were taken of the length of time (in months) that the parents of each young adult had spent in paid employment when they were children. These were obtained for each of four developmental stages in the children's lives: under one; one to five; six to ten; and 11 to 15.
- For mothers, a distinction was made between time spent in part-time work and time spent in full-time work.

The retrospective data did not include information on wages, labour income or expenditure. However, information was gathered on each interviewee's occupation. This meant that an index of occupational prestige – the Hope-Goldthorpe (HG) index – could be applied to all the jobs that parents had held when their children were growing up. This, in turn, provided a measure that could be used to control for the earnings potential of each parent.[5]

The main sample

The sampling strategy yielded a main sample consisting of 1,263 individuals who:
- were aged 16 or more and were born between 1970 and 1981;
- did not have serious health problems or disabilities;
- were living with their biological, adoptive or step-parent(s) for at least one year during the first seven waves of the panel study (1991–97);
- had mothers from whom complete employment histories had been gathered,

covering their childhoods (as well as information covering other variables).

We imposed this last condition so that, by construction, we would have full information on all the key variables for our analysis.

The restricted sample

The condition that children should have spent at least a year with their biological, adoptive or step-parent(s) during the panel study was imposed so that data on family background from the parents' records could be reliably matched with data on their child. However, such a condition would create the potential for sample selection bias if there were unobserved factors affecting young adult outcomes that had also affected the chances that children would be living with their parents. For that reason we also constructed a restricted sample (RS), consisting of individuals from the main sample (MS) who were living with at least one parent when aged 16–17.[6] The justification for doing this was that 95 per cent of all young people aged 16–17 live at home with their parents. Thus, the restricted sample (consisting of 884 individuals) was likely to be a random sample, representative of the whole population of that age, from which any selection bias had been eliminated.

Sibling differences

Both the 'main' and the 'restricted' samples were used to estimate the effects of parental employment patterns on children's achievements, using controls based on observed differences between siblings. In the main sample there were 359 households with two or more siblings (or half-siblings), which yielded a total of 793 individuals and allowed a

Table 3.1: The four samples				
	Main sample (MS)	Restricted sample (RS)	Siblings in main sample (SMS)	Siblings in restricted sample (SRS)
Number of individuals	1263	884	793	509
Number of siblings comparisons	–	–	516	304

Source: British Household Panel Survey, 1991–97.

maximum of 516 sibling comparisons in each wave of data. The restricted sample included 238 households with two or more siblings, yielding 509 individuals and 304 sibling comparisons. Table 3.1 summarises the number of individuals used in each of the four samples under study.

Personal traits

Just under half the young adults in each of the four samples were women. The ages of the young adults in the main sample (MS) and siblings in the main sample (SMS) ranged between 16 and 27, with an average just above 21. The age range of 16 to 24 for young people in the restricted sample (RS) and for siblings in the restricted sample (SRS) was narrower, with an average of less than 20. The average year of birth for people in the main sample was 1976 compared with 1977 for those in the restricted sample. The average age differences between siblings in the SMS and SRS samples were 3.1 and 2.7 years, respectively. Only 15 per cent of age differences in the SMS and 7 per cent in the SRS were greater than five years.

Parents' employment

Young people were only included in the samples if complete information was available about their mother's employment patterns during their childhood together with other background variables relating to their mothers. However, one in six young people had no 'father-figure'[7] present during the seven 'panel' years who could be interviewed. In addition there were one in six for whom information about their father's working histories was not available. This was either because the father was not present when retrospective information was collected during the third wave of the BHPS, or because it subsequently proved impossible to construct a complete work history. However, rather than exclude individuals when their father's work history was not available, it was decided to maximise the sample by including them and using indicator variables to take account of the missing information.

As expected, fathers had on average been active in the labour market for 90 per cent of the first 16 years of their children's lives – an average of 14.6 years. In other words, they averaged about a month of non-employment for each of those years (Table 3.2).

By contrast, mothers were in either full or part-time paid employment for an average of eight years during the first 16 years of their children's lives. Moreover, there was a clear relationship between mothers' employment

15

Table 3.2: Average values of parents' employment variables

Variable	Estimating sample			
	MS	RS	SMS	SRS
*Father's employment***				
child aged <12 months (months)	11.5	11.5	11.6	11.6
child aged 1–5 (years)	4.4	4.4	4.5	4.6
child aged 6–10 (years)	4.6	4.6	4.6	4.6
child aged 11–15 (years)	4.6	4.5	4.6	4.7
*Mother's employment**				
child aged <12 months (months)	2.1	2.1	1.8	1.9
child aged 1–5 (years)	1.5	1.5	1.3	1.3
child aged 6–10 (years)	2.7	2.7	2.6	2.6
child aged 11–15 (years)	3.6	3.7	3.7	3.9
*Mother's part-time employment**				
child aged <12 months (months)	0.9	1.0	0.9	1.1
child aged 1–5 (years)	0.9	0.9	0.9	0.9
child aged 6–10 (years)	1.7	1.7	1.7	1.8
child aged 11–15 (years)	2.2	2.3	2.3	2.6
*Mother's full-time employment**				
child aged <12 (months)	1.2	1.1	0.9	0.8
child aged 1–5 (years)	0.6	0.5	0.4	0.3
child aged 6–10 (years)	1.0	1.0	0.8	0.7
child aged 11–15 (years)	1.5	1.5	1.3	1.3
n =	1263	884	793	509

* Computed on all observations.

** Computed on cases with non-missing father's employment information only.

Numbers adjusted to one decimal place.

patterns and the ages of their children. Figure 3.1 shows that mothers in the main sample worked an average of only two months in the first year of their children's lives. Between the child's first and sixth birthday, the average was around 17 months. During their children's primary-school years, mothers' time in paid employment increased to an average of 32 months. Then, during their children's remaining five years of compulsory schooling, they worked for an average of 44 months.

Another way of looking at how mothers' employment varied with the ages of their children can be seen in Figure 3.2.

This shows how the proportion of mothers

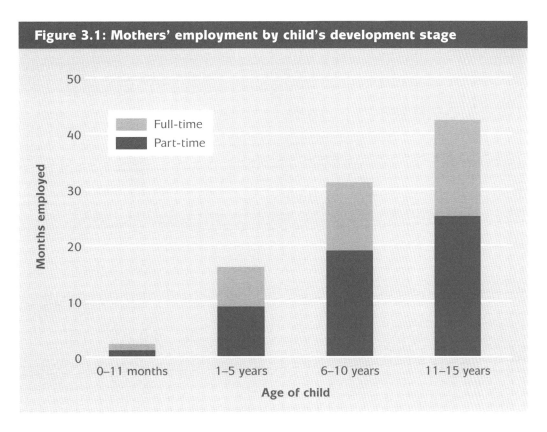

Figure 3.1: Mothers' employment by child's development stage

who were in paid work for at least one month grew from 28 per cent in the first year of children's lives to 93 per cent when their children were aged 11 to 15. In other words, only 7 per cent of the mothers in our samples undertook no paid work at any time while their children were at secondary school. The most striking growth in mothers' labour force participation occurred in part-time work, where there was a four-fold increase from an average of 14 per cent in children's first year of life to 55 per cent when children were adolescents.

The BHPS work history data made it possible to break down maternal employment by occupation, using five broad groups.[8] Thus, seven per cent of mothers in the main sample who were employed when their children were aged under 12 months were managers, 10 per

cent were professionals, 29 per cent were non-manual workers, 33 per cent were manual workers and 21 per cent were unskilled (Table 3.3). Across all the samples and in each developmental stage, it can also be seen that a high proportion of mothers were employed in manual and unskilled jobs. So much so, that if we add non-manual occupations such as nurses and secretaries, about 85 per cent of employed mothers were in relatively low-paid jobs. There was little variation in the occupational distribution of employed mothers at each stage of their children's development. Unskilled occupations were slightly under-represented among mothers of children aged six or older, and slightly over-represented among mothers working when their children were aged one to five.

Table 3.3: Mothers' employment patterns, by occupation and by their children's developmental stage (per cent)

Occupation and developmental stage	Estimating sample			
	MS	RS	SMS	SRS
Child aged <12 months				
Managerial	7.1	6.7	9.1	7.5
Professional	9.9	12.6	14.5	15.6
Non-manual	29.2	28.9	21.6	23.9
Manual	33.2	33.6	35.2	35.8
Unskilled	20.6	18.2	19.6	17.2
Total	100.0	100.0	100.0	100.0
Child aged 1–5				
Managerial	5.5	4.9	4.0	3.9
Professional	8.3	10.1	10.6	14.0
Non-manual	28.7	28.2	27.8	27.4
Manual	34.4	35.1	36.3	35.8
Unskilled	23.1	21.7	20.3	18.9
Total	100.0	100.0	100.0	100.0
Child aged 6–10				
Managerial	4.5	3.5	3.5	2.8
Professional	8.9	10.7	11.2	14.4
Non-manual	31.9	30.8	31.3	30.5
Manual	35.8	38.0	36.4	36.7
Unskilled	18.9	17.0	17.6	15.6
Total	100.0	100.0	100.0	100.0
Child aged 11–15				
Managerial	5.2	4.3	4.3	2.8
Professional	8.8	10.1	10.5	12.6
Non-manual	34.9	34.0	34.9	35.1
Manual	32.5	34.8	33.5	34.3
Unskilled	18.6	16.8	16.8	15.2
Total	100.0	100.0	100.0	100.0
n =	1263	884	793	509

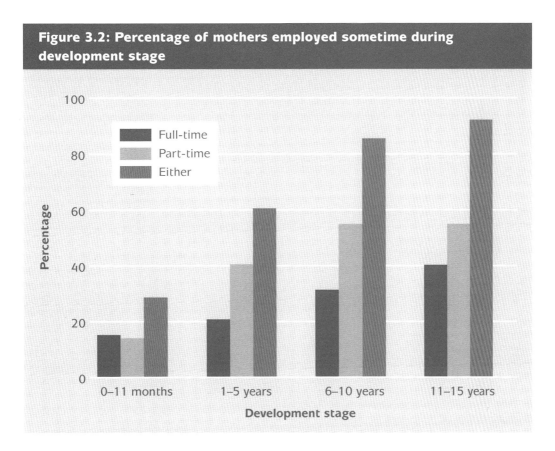

Figure 3.2: Percentage of mothers employed sometime during development stage

Parents' education and occupational status

As previously discussed, parents' own educational achievements may well reflect their attitudes towards education and the cultural environment where children are raised.

Table 3.4 shows that more than a quarter of mothers and a third of fathers in the main sample had no academic qualifications while less than one in ten parents held a university degree.

Table 3.5 shows that the average score for occupational prestige using the Hope-Goldthorpe (HG) index was much higher for fathers than for mothers when their children were aged under 16. This was a further reflection of men's higher position on the occupational pay and status ladders compared with women.

Family structure

Size

Many researchers have observed a connection between family size and educational attainment (Zajonc and Markus 1975; Lindert 1977; Stafford 1987). Their findings suggest that family size may be an important determinant of young people's achievements because parents' time and money are likely to be spread more thinly as the number of children in a family increases. In view of this, our analysis took account of the number of brothers and sisters that each young adult had. It also included a variable taking notice of whether the respondent was an only child and whether he or she was the first born in their family. This showed that approximately 7 per cent of the young people were only children,

Table 3.4: Parents' educational qualifications (percentages according to highest qualification held)

	Estimating sample	
	MS	RS
Mother's education		
No qualification (base)	29.2	26.7
Less than O-level	11.6	11.3
O-level	22.5	22.7
A-level	7.4	7.8
Higher vocational qualifications (eg. nursing and teaching)	21.0	22.6
Higher qualifications	8.3	8.9
Total	100.0	100.0
Father's education		
No qualification (base)	36.4	35.3
Less than O-level	6.8	6.0
O-level	15.5	15.3
A-level	9.3	10.2
Higher vocational qualifications (eg. nursing and teaching)	23.5	24.0
Higher qualifications	8.5	9.2
Total	100.0	100.0
n =	1263	884

Table 3.5: Average measures of occupational status using the Hope-Goldthorpe (HG) index

	Estimating sample			
	MS	RS	SMS	SRS
Mothers	37.6	38.1	38.0	38.5
Fathers	44.4	44.9	44.8	45.4
Father not interviewed	*17.7%*	*18%*	*15.8%*	*16.7%*
Information on father's employment missing	*34.0%*	*34.5%*	*31.9%*	*34.99%*
n =	1263	884	793	509

and that 40 per cent were first-born (Table 3.6). The average number of brothers and sisters was between one and two.

Age of parents
The ages of parents at the time their children were born were also included in the analysis as possible explanatory variables because older parents would tend to be more established in their working lives and careers, and more likely to enjoy higher pay and job status. The average age for mothers when their (main sample) child was born was 26 (Table 3.6). Fathers were approximately two years older. About 11 per cent of young adults in the study had been born when their mothers were aged 21 or under, but only 5 per cent had

fathers who were that young. Another 2 to 4 per cent had mothers who were 35 or over and 5 to 6 per cent had fathers who were 37 or over at the time of their birth.

Experience of life in a lone-parent family
About one in four young people in both the main and restricted samples had experienced life in a lone-parent family (Table 3.6). Of these, some 45 per cent had lived in a lone-parent family when they were under the age of six. The proportion of young adults in the sibling samples who had experienced life in a lone-parent family was very slightly lower, at about one in five. But the proportion who had done so by the age of six was again around 45 per cent.

Table 3.6: Family structure

Variable	Estimating sample			
	MS	RS	SMS	SRS
First-born (per cent)	44.0	41.0	41.0	40.0
Only child (per cent)	7.0	7.0	–	–
Age of mother at birth (years)	26.36	26.41	26.22	26.33
Age of father at birth (years)	28.70	28.65	28.56	28.51
Ever in single-parent family (per cent)				
child aged <12 months	2.0	3.0	2.0	2.0
child aged 1–5	8.0	8.0	7.0	8.0
child aged 6–10	8.0	9.0	7.0	7.0
child aged 11–15	5.0	5.0	5.0	5.0
Ever in stepfamily (per cent)				
child aged <12 months	0.3	0.4	0.1	0.2
child aged 1–5	4.0	4.0	3.0	3.0
child aged 6–10	6.0	6.0	4.0	4.0
child aged 11–15	4.0	5.0	4.0	4.0
n =	1263	884	793	509

Experience of life in a stepfamily

About 15 per cent of the young adults in the main sample and 12 per cent of those in the restricted sample had spent time in a stepfamily (bottom panel in Table 3.6). This meant that some 60 per cent of those who had lived with a lone parent had also experienced life in a stepfamily.

Outcomes among young people

Educational qualifications

The main measure of educational attainment for this study was whether young people achieved an A-level pass or higher qualification.[9] This was applied by taking the highest qualification that young people had achieved in the last year in which they were interviewed. As it is rare to obtain A-levels before the age of 18, we limited the estimating sample for this outcome to young people who were that age or older. On that basis, almost 62 per cent in the main sample (and 63 per cent of the restricted sample) had acquired at least one A-level (see Table 3.7). If this proportion seems high, it should be remembered that it includes those with higher

vocational qualifications, such as teaching and nursing qualifications, City and Guilds certificate, Higher Certificates/Diplomas and University Diplomas, many of whom may not have gained A-levels. Interestingly, however, the analysis found a substantial proportion of families where educational attainments differed between siblings. For example, there were as many as 40 per cent of families where one sibling had A-level qualifications and a brother or sister did not.

Unemployment and other economic inactivity

This outcome was defined as young people not being in paid employment, full-time education, looking after children, or taking part in a government training programme.[10] As Table 3.7 shows, the inactivity rate was around 7 per cent in any one year for individuals in the main samples, and about 6 per cent for the rather younger members of the restricted samples.

Mental health problems

Our measure of mental health problems was young people experiencing a high level of psychological distress, derived from

Table 3.7: Outcomes among young people (percentages)

| Variable | Estimating sample | | | |
	MS	RS	SMS	SRS
A-level qualifications or higher[a]	61.7	62.9	64.1	66.5
Economic inactivity[a]	7.5	6.0	6.7	5.9
High level of mental stress[a]	22.5	22.1	23.2	23.5
Early birth (women only)[a]	2.3	2.0	2.9	2.6

a = Computed on all relevant sample-specific and outcome-specific observations.

questions about a set of subjective indicators of personal well-being (known as the GHQ 12 point measure).

These indicators relate to:

- loss of concentration;
- loss of sleep;
- playing a useful role;
- ability to make decisions;
- feeling constantly under strain;
- problems overcoming difficulties;
- enjoyment of day-to-day activities;
- ability to face problems;
- unhappiness or feeling depressed;
- loss of confidence;
- belief in self-worth;
- general happiness.

More than one in five young adults exhibited psychological distress according to this measure (see Table 3.7).

Early childbearing

This outcome was defined as young women having given birth before their twenty-first birthday. A decision was taken to focus on young mothers, because relatively few men in the sample had become fathers before their twenty-first birthday and lived with their children. Table 3.7 shows that, on average, 2 per cent of previously childless women aged 16–21 in the main and restricted samples had a child each year, and almost 3 per cent in the samples of siblings.[11] As would be expected, the rate at which young women gave birth for the first time was highest for those aged 20 and lowest for 16-year-olds.

The analysis

The statistical techniques applied in this study were broadly those of multivariate regression. In other words, when assessing the impact of parental employment on the outcomes for young people, the analysis applied statistical controls for the other relevant variables described in this chapter, including personal traits, parents' education, parents' age at time of birth and parents' occupational status. The results of the analysis treating each young adult as an individual observation, using the main and restricted samples, are reported as the **between family estimates** that can be compared with the results from previous research studies. They are primarily based on comparisons across families. The analysis of the relationship between the differences in parental employment and the outcomes between brothers or sisters are reported as the **sibling difference estimates**. They use the two sibling samples (see above) and only make comparisons *within families*.

In calculating the *between family estimates*, parents' average occupational prestige scores and educational qualifications were used to control for the earnings potential of parents when they were in paid employment. Failure to apply this control would have risked confusing any effects of parental employment on their children's outcomes with the well-known association between parents' educational (and other) 'endowments' and those of their children. Even so, for reasons discussed in Chapter 2, this may be an imperfect control. Strong assumptions would still be needed before the results could be interpreted as showing a causal relationship between mothers' paid work and their children's outcomes as young adults. The estimates using *sibling differences* are able to overcome many of these inherent difficulties because – by definition – they include robust controls for parents' endowments, their earnings potential and any other unobserved family influences that are shared by both siblings. Discussion of the study's findings in the next chapter will, therefore, focus largely on the *sibling difference estimates*, because they require fewer assumptions to be interpreted as indicating a causal relationship. Since both types of estimates attempt to control for other influences on young people's outcomes, the measured 'effects' should be interpreted as the impact of reducing the amount of parental time available for their children, holding earnings and other family income constant. In other words, the measured effects are *not* the net effect of less parental time, but of more earnings.

It will also be seen that all the estimates are presented in the same format: namely, an assessment of 'marginal effects' on the outcomes for a young adult after controls have been applied for other variables (calculated at the average values for the other variables). For example, the *between family estimates* from the main sample point to a negative, marginal effect of 5.1 percentage points on the probability of young people achieving A-level qualifications if their mothers worked full-time for an additional year when they were aged between one and five (see Table 4.1). Analysis of the sibling comparison sample points to a larger negative, marginal effect of 12.3 percentage points. What this means is that young people in the sibling sample whose mothers worked full-time when they were pre-schoolers for the baseline, average amount of time, had a 62 per cent probability of achieving an A-level, but this fell to 50 per cent for those whose mothers had worked full-time for an additional year. In other words, children whose mothers worked full-time for longer periods during their pre-school years were less likely to obtain higher qualifications than children whose mothers worked for fewer months, or not at all.

4 | The effects of parents' employment

This chapter considers the relationships between parents' employment and each of the study outcomes in turn. It will be seen from the outset that there is little discussion of the effects of undertaking paid work during a child's first year of life because it proved impossible to estimate them with any precision.[12] It is worth noting, however, that when data for children's first year of life were combined with those for children aged one to five, the resulting estimates proved very similar to those for the one to five age group alone.

The discussion will focus on the results relating to the pre-school years of parents' employment for three main reasons:

- When children are in school there is less conflict between parents' time in paid employment and time spent with their children. Indeed, the children are not available at home for a large part of the day.
- Parents may have very limited knowledge of their children's endowments before they enter school, making it less likely that their employment decisions will be affected. Parents' working arrangements seem more likely to be influenced once children are aged five and over because they have more information about their child's endowments, not least through school. If so, we cannot interpret the estimated associations as 'effects'.
- The pre-school years are particularly important for a child's development.

In the interests of full reporting, we show results that include parents' employment from all four developmental stages. But the measured effects of parents' employment in the pre-school years remained similar when measures of parents' employment at ages above five were omitted from the analysis.

Mothers' employment

Educational attainment

We found evidence of an adverse effect on the chances of children achieving at least one A-level if their mothers had worked when they were aged one to five (Figure 4.1). As previewed in the previous chapter, the *between family estimates* suggested that an additional year of full-time work was associated with a 5.1 percentage point lower likelihood of children achieving at least one A-level by the time they were young adults. The *sibling difference estimates* showed a considerably larger reduction of probability of 12.3 percentage points. Indeed, the negative impact of full-time maternal employment when children were aged one to five on educational attainment proved relatively robust across all the estimation methods and samples. Table 4.1 shows that the impact of a one-year increase of mothers' full-time employment when her child was a pre-schooler ranged between a 5 per cent reduction in the probability of achieving one A-level in the *between family estimates* from the main sample to a 20 percentage point reduction among siblings from the restricted sample.

The sibling comparisons in the main sample also pointed to a much smaller, although significant, reduction of six percentage points in the probability of achieving A-level qualifications linked to an additional year of mother's part-time employment during the pre-school years. The *between family estimates*, using the main sample, showed no effects that were statistically significant. However, this could reflect failure to control adequately for family background in these estimates (see Chapter 3).[14]

Table 4.1: Effects of an additional year of childhood maternal part-time and full-time employment on the probability of achieving A-level or more, by developmental stage[12] (absolute ratios of coefficient to standard error are shown in parentheses)

Mother's employment	Between family estimates, percentages		Sibling difference estimates, percentages	
	MS	RS	SMS	SRS
Baseline	61.7	62.9	64.1	66.2
Part-time employment:				
Child aged <12 months	*5.3*	*3.7*	*-1.1*	*2.7*
(+1 month)	*(1.70)*	*(0.95)*	*(0.20)*	*(0.68)*
Child aged 1–5	-1.1	-1.3	-6.2	-10.4
(+1 year)	(0.85)	(0.77)	(2.00)	(1.94)
Child aged 6–10	-0.4	0.5	0.9	-0.7
(+1 year)	(0.01)	(0.50)	(0.58)	(0.28)
Child aged 11–15	1.1	1.1	-1.0	-2.1
(+1 year)	(1.70)	(1.38)	(0.59)	(0.80)
Full-time employment:				
Child aged <12 months	*2.5*	*3.2*	*5.1*	*-1.6*
(+1 month)	*(1.23)*	*(1.16)*	*(0.75)*	*(0.15)*
Child aged 1–5	-5.1	-9.7	-12.3	-19.5
(+1 year)	(1.68)	(2.23)	(3.10)	(2.55)
Child aged 6–10	-1.1	1.5	13.7	7.8
(+1 year)	(0.66)	(0.73)	(2.86)	(0.94)
Child aged 11–15	2.5	2.1	-0.5	-4.5
(+1 year)	(2.67)	(1.77)	(0.17)	(1.10)
n =	1026	647	381	187

It is, of course, possible that the impact of full-time employment when children were aged one to five may have differed between mothers in better-paid jobs and mothers in poorer jobs. Better-paid mothers might, for example, have been able to afford better-quality child care or they might have allocated their time when not working differently. To test this, we divided mothers between those whose highest qualifications were above A-level (about 30 per cent of the total) and those with qualifications of A-level or lower. We then examined whether the impacts of each type of employment at each stage in children's development differed significantly (in a statistical sense) between the two groups.

Overall, they did not. But there was some evidence in the *sibling difference estimates* (main sample) that the negative effect of full-

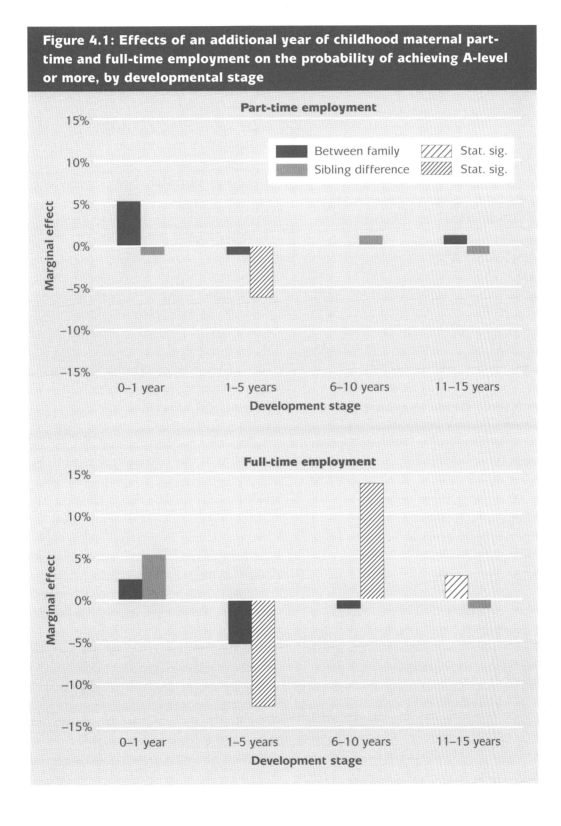

Figure 4.1: Effects of an additional year of childhood maternal part-time and full-time employment on the probability of achieving A-level or more, by developmental stage

time employment when children were aged one to five was smaller for more-educated mothers, although the difference lay on the margins of statistical significance. And even then, the adverse effects for young people with more highly educated mothers who had worked full-time for longer periods remained substantial.

The *sibling difference estimates* from the main sample (Figure 4.1) suggested that an additional year of mothers' full-time employment when children were aged six to ten served to increase the probability of their later achieving an A-level or higher qualifications by 14 percentage points. This association was, not, however, very robust: it remained positive in the *between family estimates* and among siblings in the restricted sample, but ceased to be statistically significant. As noted earlier, the association at these ages could reflect a *response* of mother's employment to a child doing well in school (ie. a response to child endowments), rather than an *effect* of mother's employment. The reversal of direction could also reflect the fact that there is less conflict between parents' time in paid employment and the time available to be with their children when children spend a large part of the day in school.

In summary, the *sibling difference estimates* suggested that longer periods of full-time employment by mothers when their children were pre-schoolers tended to reduce their educational attainments – and that this was because they had less time to spend with them during those formative years. While there is some suggestion that continuing to work full time when children were aged six to ten offset some of this negative impact, it was also apparent that children would have done even better if their mothers had delayed working full-time until they reached the age of six. Mothers working part-time for longer periods when children were aged between one and five also affected their child's educational attainment, but the negative effect was much smaller.

Economic inactivity

Given the reduction in young people's educational attainment associated with longer periods of full-time employment by mothers when children were aged one to five, the analysis might have been expected to reveal a similar pattern in relation to the chances of being unemployed or otherwise economically inactive. However, as Figure 4.2 shows, the picture that emerged was not clear-cut. Although the estimates based on sibling differences showed an adverse effect (increasing the probability of economic inactivity by 2.3 percentage points), it only reached the margins of statistical significance.[15] There was also a lack of supporting evidence of a corresponding effect among siblings from the restricted sample.

For the reasons suggested earlier, the measured 'effects' from parents' employment at older ages should be treated with a degree of caution. There is some evidence that longer periods of employment by mothers when their children were older were associated with a reduced likelihood that children would be economically inactive as young adults. For example, the *sibling difference* analysis suggested that an additional year of part-time employment by mothers when their children were aged six to ten reduced the probability of being economically inactive by 0.5 percentage points. Mothers' employment when their children were aged 11–15 was also

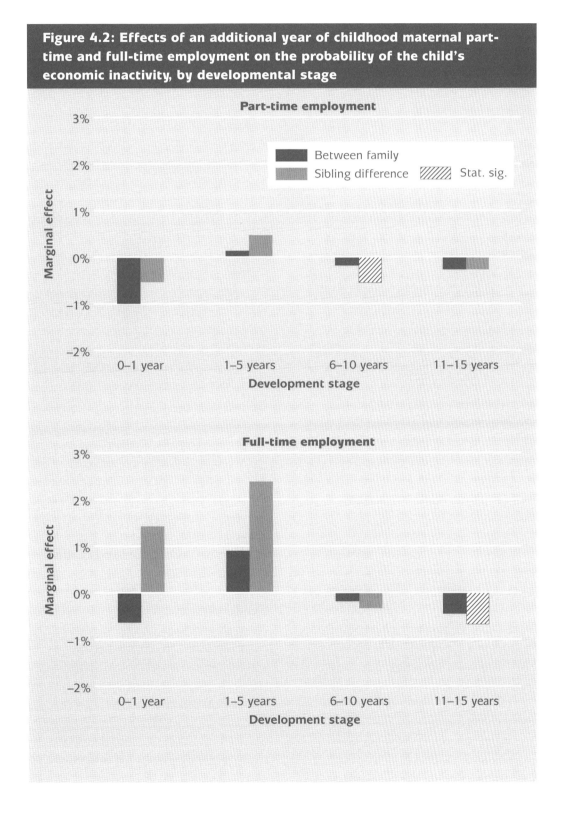

Figure 4.2: Effects of an additional year of childhood maternal part-time and full-time employment on the probability of the child's economic inactivity, by developmental stage

associated with a lower risk of subsequent unemployment. For example, an additional year of mothers' full-time work lowered the probability of economic inactivity by 0.6 percentage points.

Mental health

The findings for mental health outcomes contain parallels with those for educational attainment. There were adverse effects of mothers' full-time working when children were pre-schoolers (Figure 4.3). Thus, an additional year of full-time employment by mothers when their children were aged one to five increased the probability of experiencing psychological distress as a young adult by about 5 percentage points in the sibling differences sample, and 3 percentage points in the *between family estimates*. Although large in relation to the baseline average, these effects were on the margins of statistical significance. Interestingly, however, the *sibling difference estimates* suggested that longer periods of *part-time* employment when children were aged one to five were associated with a lower risk of later psychological distress.

An association of more full-time employment by mothers when their children were aged six to ten with a lower risk of psychological distress (by about 3 percentage points) was evident from all the estimates. This is, again, difficult to interpret because a mother's employment at these ages may be responding to her knowledge of her child's endowments.

Early childbearing

The analysis comparing sibling outcomes suggested that the amount of time mothers spent in part-time employment had little effect on the probability of their daughter giving birth at an early age. Full-time employment was, by contrast, significantly related to the chances that daughters' would have a child by age 21 (see Figure 4.4). An additional year of maternal full-time employment during children's pre-school years was seen to reduce the annual probability of early childbearing by more than 2 percentage points (*sibling difference estimates*). This is a large (although not precisely measured) effect considering that the baseline average for annual birth probability was only 3 per cent.

A surprising result from the *sibling difference estimates* is that longer periods of full-time employment by mothers when their daughters were in primary school were associated with higher annual chances of young motherhood, by about 3 per cent (rising to 5 per cent in the restricted sample). Although this is a relatively large association, the mechanisms that might explain it are unclear. It might be assumed that any loss of parental control associated with a mother working full-time would mainly operate when the daughter was a teenager. However the findings for mothers working full-time for longer periods when their children were aged 11 to 15 work in the opposite direction.

Gender differences

The study attempted to discover whether differences could be detected in outcomes between young men and young women in relation to the effects of mothers' employment patterns. However, it proved impossible to make hard and fast statements because the number of sibling comparisons in the restricted sample was too small to support a serious analysis by gender. Even in

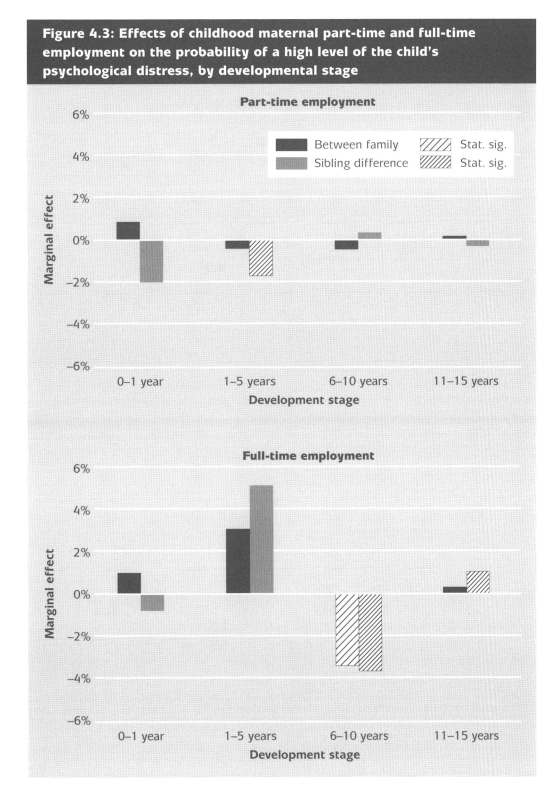

Figure 4.3: Effects of childhood maternal part-time and full-time employment on the probability of a high level of the child's psychological distress, by developmental stage

Figure 4.4: Effects of an additional year of childhood maternal part-time and full-time employment on the annual probability of early childbearing, by developmental stage

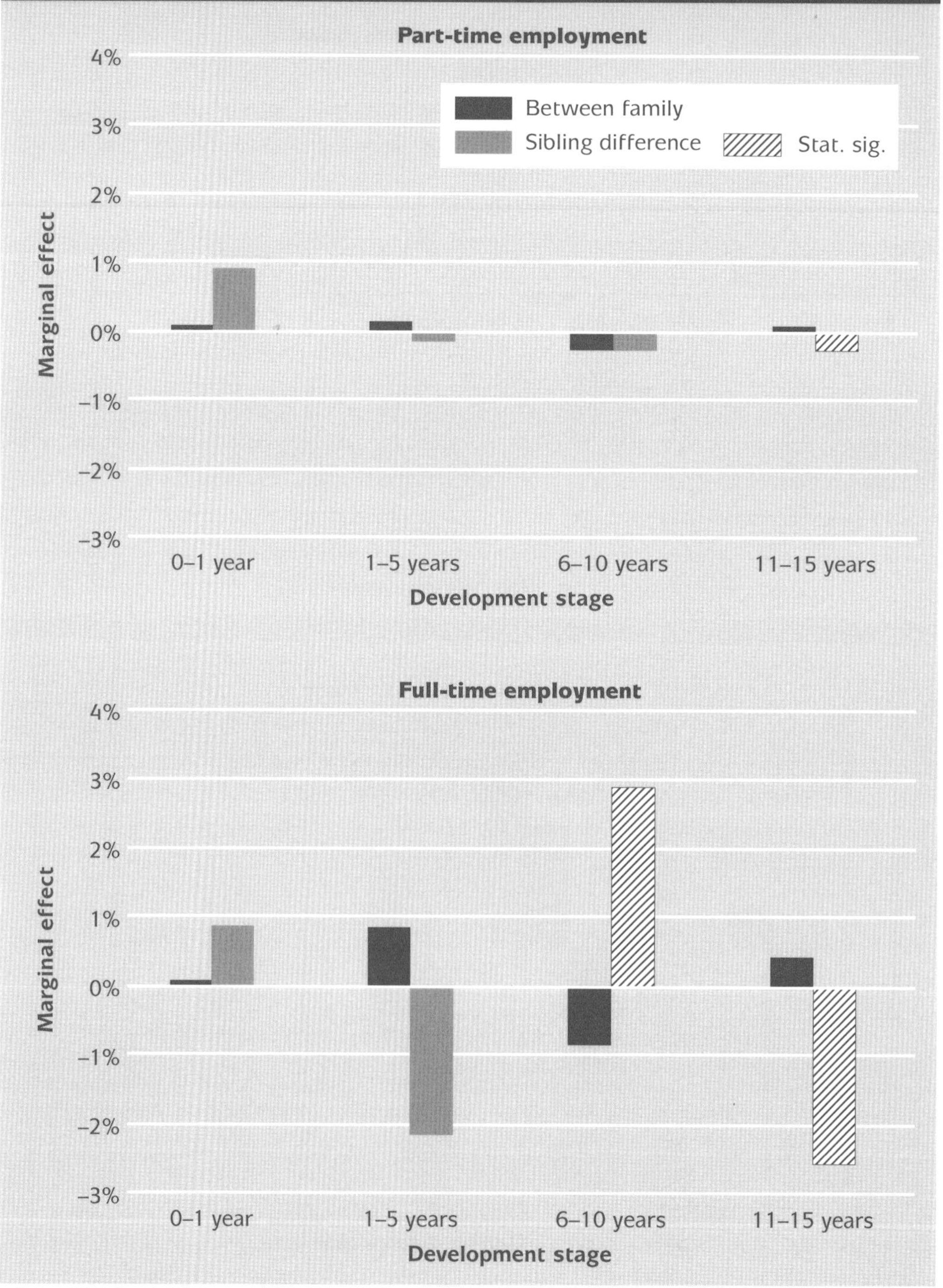
Part-time employment
4%
3%
2%
1%
0%
-1%
-2%
-3%
Marginal effect
Between family
Sibling difference
Stat. sig.
0–1 year
1–5 years
6–10 years
11–15 years
Development stage
Full-time employment
4%
3%
2%
1%
0%
-1%
-2%
-3%
Marginal effect
0–1 year
1–5 years
6–10 years
11–15 years
Development stage

the main sample, the sibling comparisons available for analysis of educational attainment amounted to only 117 brothers and 86 sisters.

Effects of fathers' employment

The study examined the effects of fathers' employment patterns on their children's outcomes as young adults. However, a number of limiting factors described in Chapter 3 need to be borne in mind when considering the results:

- No information on biological fathers or stepfathers was available for one in six of the young adults in our samples.
- For another sixth of young adults we could not recover any information on fathers' employment patterns during their childhood.
- Some of the fathers we identified in the panel survey were stepfathers who were not in the household throughout the young adult's childhood. Our analysis only accounts for this through indicator variables for experience of a stepfamily.
- The vast majority of fathers in our samples were employed most of the time – an average of 14.6 years of employment in the first 16 years of their children's lives. The lack of any substantial variations in working patterns across families and over time made it unlikely from the outset that any differences in the outcomes for young adults would be associated with father's employment in a way that was statistically significant.
- We measured the periods of time that fathers spent in employment rather than the time and energy they devoted to their children. Fathers who devoted an identical amount of time to paid work, might have

devoted substantially different amounts of time to their children and to activities that were relevant to their future achievements.

Educational attainment
We found some evidence of an effect of fathers' employment when his children were pre-schoolers on the probability of achieving one A-level or more. The *sibling difference estimates* suggested that longer periods of employment when children were aged under six reduced their educational attainment, but this effect could not be precisely estimated in the restricted sibling sample. (The detailed results can be found in the web-site annex to this report www.iser.essex.ac.uk/jrf/ermij/annex.php)

Economic inactivity
An extra month of employment by fathers during children's first year of life reduced the child's probability of being economically inactive as a young adult by between 0.5 and 1 percentage points a year. This effect was robust across the different estimators and samples. However, there was no consistent evidence of any relationship between fathers' employment and their children's chances of being unemployed at later stages in their development.

Mental health
Longer periods of employment by fathers when their children were aged one to five reduced the chances that children would experience high levels of psychological distress as young adults. A possible explanation would be that employed fathers had fewer financial worries when their children were growing up. Both the *sibling difference* and the *between family estimates*

suggested that an additional year employed when their children were aged one to five reduced the probability of distress by 2 to 4 percentage points.

Early childbearing

More months of fathers' employment when their children were aged one to five was associated with a lower likelihood that daughters would first give birth when 21 or younger, but this association was not statistically significant. In contrast, according to the *sibling difference estimates*, more employment in his children's first year of life was associated with a larger probability of early childbearing. The mechanism behind this association is, however, unclear.

5 | Other influences

The study examined a number of other factors that might have influenced young people's outcomes, aside from the time that parents spent in paid work when they were children. These included the young person's personal traits and family structure: for example, whether children had spent part of their upbringing in a lone-parent family. The results are reported in Figures 5.1 to 5.8 (with full details available on the web-site annex).

Personal traits

There was no significant difference between young men and young women in the samples in terms of the percentages who achieved A-level qualifications or better. However, young men were more likely to be economically inactive and less likely to experience high levels of psychological distress than young women (see Figure 5.1).

Using the *between family estimates*, it was possible to examine whether the levels of educational attainment and other outcomes varied for the different cohorts of children born in particular years. Figure 5.1 suggests that those born more recently were more likely than earlier cohorts to reach A-level standard and less likely to be economically inactive. However, they were also more likely to experience high levels of psychological distress. There was no statistically significant effect between cohorts for early childbearing.

As might be expected, Figure 5.2 shows that the likelihood that young people would hold an A-level or equivalent qualification increased with age. So, in the case of daughters, did the chances of giving birth for the first time. The chances of experiencing psychological distress were also greater once

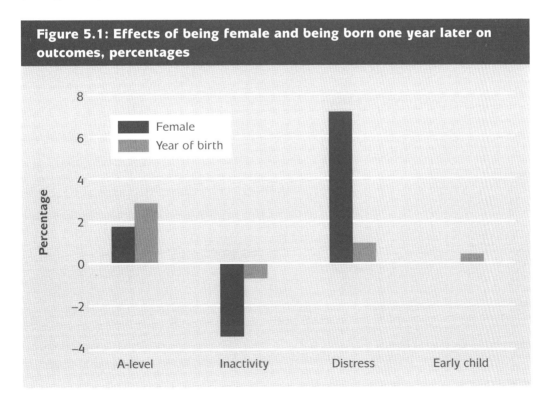

Figure 5.1: Effects of being female and being born one year later on outcomes, percentages

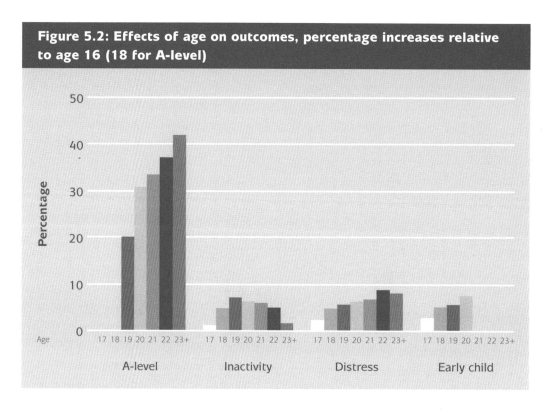

Figure 5.2: Effects of age on outcomes, percentage increases relative to age 16 (18 for A-level)

young people had reached their early 20s. The risk of unemployment was greatest at the age of 19 and then tended to decline.[16]

Parents' educational attainment

The relationship between parents' educational attainment and outcomes for their children can only be measured using the *between family estimates*. Figures 5.3 and 5.4 show that – as might be expected – the resulting correlations were large and statistically significant in the case of young people's educational attainment and economic inactivity. However, they also proved to be small and insignificant for psychological distress and early childbearing.

Parents' occupational prestige

Not surprisingly, parents' educational attainment was strongly associated with their

average occupational prestige measured using the Hope-Goldthorpe (HG) index. However, the analysis found that, in addition to any effects of parental education, there was a strong, positive association between parents' occupational status and the probability that their children would gain A-level qualifications (Figure 5.5). This suggests a relationship between children's educational achievements and parental wealth. This interpretation was supported by the fact that the correlations applied to the *between family estimates*, but disappeared in the *sibling difference estimates*.[17] There was some evidence that children whose fathers came from higher-paid occupations were more likely to suffer from psychological distress as young adults. However the strongest and most consistent evidence of parents' occupational prestige exerting an influence concerned early

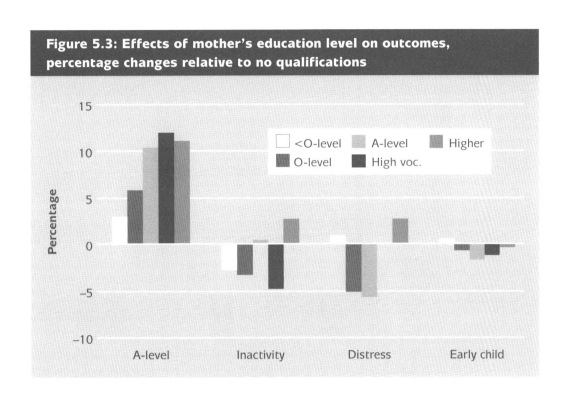

Figure 5.3: Effects of mother's education level on outcomes, percentage changes relative to no qualifications

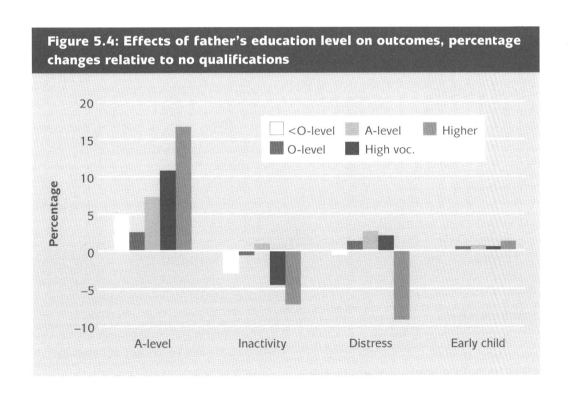

Figure 5.4: Effects of father's education level on outcomes, percentage changes relative to no qualifications

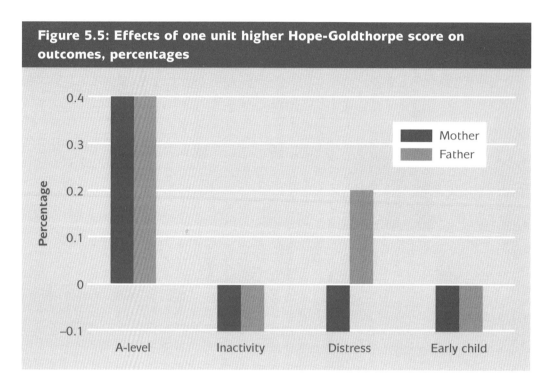

Figure 5.5: Effects of one unit higher Hope-Goldthorpe score on outcomes, percentages

childbearing. Higher occupational status for either mothers or fathers substantially reduced the chances that daughters would have given birth before the age of 21.

Age of parents

Parents' own ages when their children were born appeared to play only a small part in shaping their children's later achievements. There was little evidence of any robust relationship between a father's age at the time his child was born and any of the outcomes under study. Having a young mother (aged 21 or less at the time of birth) increased the child's probability of being economically inactive.[18]

Family size

Looking at the number of siblings in a family, it was found that having more brothers and sisters was associated with a higher probability

of being economically inactive as a young adult (Figure 5.6). The mechanism for this might well have been lower educational attainment, but the direct effects – relating qualifications to family size – could not be precisely estimated.[19] Having more brothers (but not sisters) was associated with a higher risk of early childbearing for women, although being an only child also tended to reduce the risk of an early birth. In addition, there was some evidence that being a first-born child carried an increased risk of experiencing a high level of distress in young adulthood.

Family structure

Family structure during childhood was used as a control variable for measuring the effects of parents' employment. However, it was significantly linked in its own right to outcomes in early adulthood. For example, experience of life in a lone-parent family

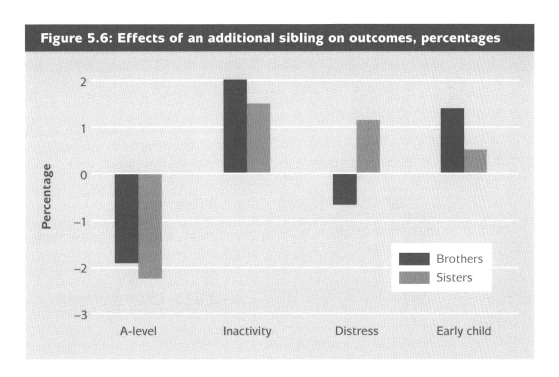

Figure 5.6: Effects of an additional sibling on outcomes, percentages

before the age of 11 was associated with a substantial reduction in the probability of achieving one or more A-levels, irrespective of the precise age at which that experience occurred (Figure 5.7). It should, however, be noted that the precision and statistical significance of the *between family estimates* vary for each development stage.

As noted in Chapter 3, some 60 per cent of young adults in the samples who had experienced life in a lone-parent family had also been part of a stepfamily. This made it difficult to separate out the effects attributable to one or other type of family with any precision. Nevertheless, when specific stepfamily variables were excluded from the analysis, the correlations between experiencing life in a lone-parent family before the age of 11 and later negative outcomes proved to be large and statistically significant.

According to these estimates, being part of a lone-parent family below the age of 11

reduced the chances of achieving A-level or higher qualifications by 10 to 15 percentage points. Further technical difficulties should be noted in relation to the figures derived from the sibling comparison samples. For instance, the effects of 'ever having been in a lone-parent family' are implausibly large. This is because the sibling difference samples were too small for this variable to produce meaningful results. In spite of the caveats described in Chapter 3, this is one occasion when greater reliance can be placed on the *between family estimates*. In addition, a forthcoming study by the authors (Ermisch and Francesconi, 2001b) confirms large, adverse effects associated with lone parenthood for all the young adult outcomes under consideration in this report, using both *between family estimates* and *sibling difference estimates*.[20]

It appeared that the adverse impact on educational attainment associated with having been part of a lone-parent family was not

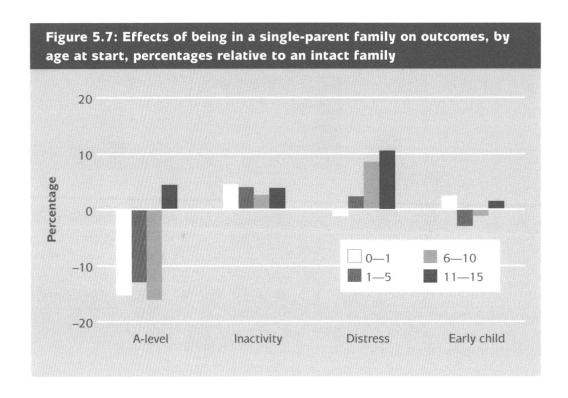

Figure 5.7: Effects of being in a single-parent family on outcomes, by age at start, percentages relative to an intact family

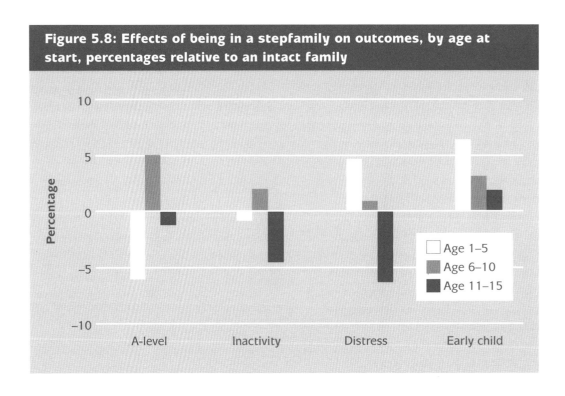

Figure 5.8: Effects of being in a stepfamily on outcomes, by age at start, percentages relative to an intact family

significantly mitigated by subsequently becoming part of a stepfamily (Figure 5.8). However, the *between family estimates* of the effects of having been part of a stepfamily on economic inactivity and psychological distress could not be measured precisely and must be treated with caution. Experience of life in a stepfamily at any age, but particularly as a pre-schooler, (Figure 5.8), and becoming part of a lone-parent family as a teenager (Figure 5.7) were both associated with a greater risk that young women would give birth before their twenty-first birthday.

6 | Conclusions

This study has used complex statistical techniques to explore the links between parents' employment histories and their children's lives and well-being as young adults. Some of its findings carry potentially important implications for public policy and for further research. A number are likely to prove controversial, arousing public debate concerning their meaning and contemporary relevance. It is, therefore, important to begin this concluding summary by being clear about some of the research's limitations:

- **Firstly**, although a large number of family background variables were controlled for in the analysis, these variables are only a few of the many factors that have a bearing on children's development. They may even be relatively minor ones, when viewed as part of a constellation of relevant factors including parents' personality, their emotional stability, parenting practices and the quality of care that children receive from their parents. The study tried to remedy this by using samples of young people that allowed comparisons between siblings from the same family. This has enabled us to eliminate any persistent family and community characteristics shared by siblings that could not otherwise be measured.
- **Secondly**, the analysis used mothers' and fathers' time spent in paid work to indicate the amount of time that they otherwise had available for their children. Using full and part-time work as a proxy in this way does not tell us how many of parents' remaining, waking hours were devoted to their children. What that means for this and most other studies that have been conducted in this area is that generalisation regarding the relative effects of different factors in

shaping children's achievements is virtually impossible.
- **Thirdly**, we have no information on the type, quantity or quality of child care used by families when mothers were employed, especially those who were in paid work when their children were of pre-school age. The quality of the alternative care those children received while their parents were at work is likely to have made an important contribution to the outcomes observed in the study. When considering the implications for current policy it should also be remembered that the availability and cost of good-quality, alternative child care may well have altered since the young adults in our sample were pre-schoolers, up to 30 years ago.

It has been important when reporting the findings from this study to explain the limits of the data available as well as its strengths. This report has referred to many instances where the available sample sizes and other factors mean the estimates obtained are imprecise, or the correlations lack statistical significance and might, therefore, have occurred as a matter of chance. One consequence is that our report has little to say about the results relating to mothers' employment when their children were babies of less than 12 months. There is, however, robust evidence to support a number of findings that can be summarised as follows:

Mothers' employment

Longer periods of full-time employment by mothers when their children were aged one to five tended to:
- reduce the child's educational attainment;
- increase the risk of unemployment and

other economic inactivity in early adulthood;
- increase the risk of experiencing psychological distress as a young adult;
- in the case of daughters, reduce the chances of becoming a mother before the age of 21.

More months of part-time employment by mothers when children were aged one to five tended to:
- reduce the child's educational attainment, but the effect was still less marked than that linked to maternal full-time employment at these ages;
- reduce the risk of later psychological distress.

Fathers' employment

The effects of fathers' employment on the outcomes studied were generally less important than those of mothers' paid work. We found that longer periods of work by fathers when their children were pre-schoolers tended to:
- reduce the risk of children becoming economically inactive as young adults;
- reduce the chances of experiencing a high level of distress in young adulthood;
- reduce the child's educational attainment.

Parents' education and occupational status

Children of more highly qualified parents tended to have:
- higher educational attainments themselves;
- a lower probability of being economically inactive as a young adult.

Higher occupational status and earnings capacity for either parent was associated with:

- higher educational attainments for their children;
- a lower risk of early childbearing for daughters.

Family structure and size

Having lived in a lone-parent family during childhood was associated with:
- lower educational achievements;
- a higher risk of early childbearing where daughters living in lone-parent families subsequently became part of a stepfamily.

Larger families and the consequences of parental resources having to be shared among several siblings may have long-term consequences. Thus, having more brothers and sisters tended to:
- increase the chance of economic inactivity;
- increase the risk of early childbearing (but only in relation to daughters with a larger number of brothers).

Policy implications

What are the implications for these estimated long-term effects on children of parents' employment for current employment, anti-poverty and childcare policies? To begin with, it has to be re-emphasised that the 'typical' child in the samples for this study was born in the mid-1970s and started school at the beginning of the 1980s. Profound changes in the lives of children and their families have occurred since then (Dex, 1999) that must be recognised in order to put the estimates into context, notably:
- an increasing number of children have experienced life apart from at least one of their parents before reaching adulthood, either because their parents separated or because their parents never lived together;

- women, particularly mothers in couples, have dramatically increased their active participation in the labour force;
- more child care is being provided outside the nuclear family. This is either happening informally, for example, through grandparents and neighbours, or through childminders, crèches and nurseries. Whether this 'outsourcing' of child care services has been accompanied by an improvement in quality is unclear.

Despite the rapid growth in mothers' employment, there has been no commensurate decline in the amount of caring work performed by families or comparable growth in the use of market-provided care (Dex, 1999). Nevertheless, these changes have occurred alongside significant changes in attitudes of mothers, families and employers towards family life and towards women's employment. For example, the British Household Panel Study has found that only 12 per cent of women and 20 per cent of men who were born between 1974 and 1981 believed that a family would suffer if the woman were in full-time employment. This compares with 36 per cent of women and 40 per cent of men in their parents' generation, who were born in the late 1940s and early 1950s. Among those born between 1974 and 1981, 25 per cent of women and 36 per cent of men believed that a pre-school child would suffer if his or her mother were employed. These figures increased among their parents' generation to 40 per cent of women and 55 per cent of men (British Household Panel Survey, 1991–1997).

Public policy, notably the Government's 'New Deal' policies on employment, has not been neutral with regard to these trends. It has actively encouraged lone mothers to take up paid work, as a means of reducing their reliance on Income Support and of moving their families out of poverty. Our evidence on occupational status supports the view that where an early return to full-time employment after childbirth helps a mother to maintain and acquire skills that increase family income, this tends to have favourable effects on her child's educational attainment.[21] However, the results also strongly suggest that, holding family income constant, pre-school children whose mothers take up full-time employment are less likely to attain A-level or equivalent qualifications as young adults, because there is less time available for their children.

If the positive effects of increasing family income are enough to offset this adverse impact on qualifications, then the policy of encouraging mothers back to full-time employment could still produce net gains for children. But policymakers pursuing this approach should, at the least, be giving urgent consideration to ways that the risks of lower educational attainment, higher unemployment and poor mental health can be reduced. The onus is on them, through evaluation, to demonstrate that an early return to full-time employment by mothers really does produce substantial and sustainable increases in family income that outweigh the negative effects.

As the matter stands, this study produces less equivocal evidence in support of a long-term pay-off from short duration, flexible employment policies such as parental leave and longer maternity leave. Entitling parents to more time with young children can be justified as a potential investment in the labour force of tomorrow.

One possibility that the present research

leaves open is that high-quality child care for pre-schoolers could mitigate any adverse effects of having a mother working full-time. At present, it is likely that well-paid mothers will have more access to such child care through the market than mothers earning lower wages. However, the only safe conclusion that policymakers should be encouraged to adopt is that more research is needed into the effects of different types of child care on children's development.

The analysis also suggests that part-time employment by mothers has fewer and smaller adverse effects on children as young adults. The one adverse effect identified was an association between longer periods of part-time employment by mothers when children were aged one to five and a reduced chance of obtaining A-level qualifications. Even then, the effect was smaller than that linked to full-time employment. It might, therefore, be better to promote mothers' part-time employment while children are in their pre-school years, even though part-time employment does not lead to the same level of longer-term gains in family income. The high proportion of mothers of young children who are already in part-time jobs suggests that, given the present cost and availability of quality child care, many women, themselves, prefer this option before their children start school.

References

Angrist, J.D. and Evans, W.N. (1998) 'Children and their parents' labor supply: evidence from exogenous variation in family size'. *American Economic Review,* 88, 450–477.

Ashenfelter, O. and Rouse, C. (1999) 'The payoff to education'. Unpublished manuscript, presented at the CEPR European Summer Symposium in Labour Economics, Ammersee, Germany.

Becker, G.S. (1981) *A treatise on the family.* Cambridge: Harvard University Press.

Blau, F.D., and Grossberg, A.J. (1992) 'Maternal labour supply and children's cognitive development'. *Review of Economics and Statistics,* 74, 474–481.

Bumpass, L.L., Raley, R.K. and Sweet, J.A. (1995) 'The changing character of stepfamilies: implications of cohabitation and non-marital childbearing'. *Demography,* 32, 425–436.

Cherlin, A.J., Kiernan, K.E. and Chase-Lansdale, P.L. (1995) 'Parental divorce in childhood and demographic outcomes in young adulthood'. *Demography,* 32, 299–318.

Cox, D.R., Fitzpatrick, R., Fletcher, A.E., Gore, S.M., Spiegelhalter, D.J. and Jones, D.R. (1994) 'Quality of life assessment: can we keep it simple?' *Journal of the Royal Statistical Society,* Series A, 155, 353–393.

Dearden, L. (1998) 'Ability, families, education and earnings in Britain'. Institute for Fiscal Studies, Working Paper No. W98/14, June.

Dex, S. (1999) ed., *Families and the labour market: trends, pressures and policies.* London: Family Policy Studies Centre.

Ermisch, J. and Francesconi, M. (1997) 'Family matters'. Centre for Economic Policy Research Discussion Paper No. 1591.

Ermisch, J.F. and Francesconi, M. (2001a) 'The increasing complexity of family relationships: lifetime experience of single motherhood and stepfamilies in Great Britain'. *European Journal of Population,* 16, 235–249.

Ermisch, J. and Francesconi, M. (2001b) 'Family structure and children's achievements'. *Journal of Population Economics,* forthcoming.

Han, W.-J., Waldfogel, J. and Brooks-Gunn, J. (1999) 'The effects of early maternal employment on later cognitive and behavioral outcomes'. Columbia University School of Social Work, unpublished paper.

Harvey, E. (1999) 'Short-term and long-term effects of early parental employment on children of the National Longitudinal Survey of Youth'. *Developmental Psychology,* 35, 445–459.

Haveman, R. and Wolfe, B. (1995) 'The determinants of children's attainments: a review of methods and findings'. *Journal of Economic Literature,* 33, 1829–1878.

Joshi, H. and Verropoulou, G. (2000) *Maternal employment and child outcomes,* Smith Institute Report.

Kiernan, K.E. (1992) 'The impact of family disruption in childhood on transitions made in young adult life'. *Population Studies,* 46, 213–234.

Kiernan, K.E. (1996) 'Lone motherhood, employment and outcomes for children'. *International Journal of Law, Policy and the Family,* 10, 233–249.

Kiernan, K.E. (1997) 'The legacy of parental divorce: social, economic and demographic experiences in adulthood'. Centre for Analysis of Social Exclusion, London School of Economics, CASEpaper 1.

Lindert, P.H. (1977) 'Sibling position and achievement'. *Journal of Human Resources,* 12, 198–219.

McHale, S.M. and Huston, T.L. (1984) 'Men and women as parents: sex role orientation, employment, and parental role with infants'. *Child Development,* 55, 1349–1361.

McLanahan, S.S. and Sandefur, G. (1994) *Growing up with a single parent.* Cambridge: Harvard University Press.

Ní Bhrolcháin, M., Chappel, R. and Diamond, I. (1994) 'Scolarité et autres caractéristiques socio-démographiques des enfants de mariages rompus'. [Educational and socio-demographic outcomes among the children of disrupted and intact marriages.] *Population,* 49,1585–1612.

Nickell, S. (1982) 'The determinants of occupational success in Britain'. Review of Economic Studies, 49, 43–53.

O'Brien, M. and Jones, D. (1999) 'Children, employment and educational attainment: an English case study'. *Cambridge Journal of Economics,* 23:599–621.

Parcel, T.L. and Menaghan, E.G. (1994) 'Early parental work, family social capital, and early childhood outcomes'. *American Journal of Sociology,* 99, 972–1009.

Secretary of State for Health (1992) *The health of the nation: a strategy for health in England* (White Paper). HMSO, London.

Stafford, F.P. (1987) 'Women's work, sibling competition, and children's school performance'. *American Economic Review,* 77, 972–980.

Weiss, Y. and Willis, R.J. (1985) 'Children as collective goods and divorce settlements'. *Journal of Labor Economics,* 3:268–292.

Zajonc, R.B. and Markus, G.B. (1975) 'Birth order and intellectual development'. *Psychological Review,* 82, 74–88.

Endnotes

1   A recent study of the 1970 birth cohort by Joshi and Verropoulou (2000) can only ascertain whether the mother was employed sometime while the child was aged under five, and work history information is missing for many mothers.

2   By focusing on individuals born in the same week, the cohort studies make it difficult, if not impossible, to use sibling differences.

3   If the birth occurred outside of a partnership and the mother partnered within one year, we assumed that the mother had moved in with the biological father (as assumed in Bumpass, Raley and Sweet (1995) and Ermisch and Francesconi (2001a)). For adopted children, we use information on the year in which they were adopted to match in the mother's family history appropriately. In 96 per cent of the cases, the children are natural children.

4   Ermisch and Francesconi (1997) experiment with other, more detailed measures of family structure, eg., the durations of different family structures. But this simple dichotomy by developmental stage performs as well in predicting educational attainment as more complex measures. In addition, Ermisch and Francesconi (2001a) find that only 242 women had a pre-partnership birth as of 1992 (wave 2), representing 0.05 per cent of all women in that survey year. Since we cannot determine whether or not they subsequently lived with the child's father, we assume that the women who formed a union within one year of the birth did so with the father. Of the 242 women who had a pre-partnership birth, 77 (32 per cent) moved in with the child's father on this assumption. Because of the small sample sizes, therefore, we cannot explore the distinction between children who experienced a family disruption when aged 0–6 and children born into a single-parent family.

5   A higher value of the Hope-Goldthorpe (HG) index means a higher occupational prestige, which is typically associated with higher paid occupations. For instance, using data for the entire BHPS sample over 1991–97, the HG index is highly correlated with observed wages.

6   The age restriction on this sample means that individuals were born between 1974 and 1981. The age range is then 16–24, while the age range in MS is 16–27.

7   The definition of 'father-figure' includes both biological fathers and stepfathers, but in this report we shall refer to them as 'fathers', for short.

8   These five categories were obtained from the 374 unit groups contained in the Standard Occupational Classification (SOC). Managerial occupations comprise managers and administrators (SOC 100 through 199); professional occupations comprise all professional occupations (SOC 200 through 299, which include teachers in primary and secondary schools); non-manual occupations comprise associate professionals, technical, clerical and secretarial occupations (SOC 300 through 491, which include nurses and secretaries); manual occupations comprise craft, personal and protective service, and sales occupations (SOC 500 through 792, which include police officers below sergeant, hairdressers, and waitresses); unskilled occupations include plant and machine operatives and other unskilled occupations (SOC 800 through 999, which include taxi and bus drivers, shelf fillers and cleaners).

9   We performed a similar analysis on higher vocational qualifications, teaching and nursing qualifications, first and higher degrees.Like the achievement of at least one A-level it proved to be strongly related to future occupational success and expected earnings. Given the similarity of the results, it is not discussed further in this report.

10 Siblings were matched on the year of observation (thus avoiding comparisons at different points of the business cycle).

11 Because having a child is inherently age-dependent, the comparisons with sisters' childbearing were made at common ages.

12 This appeared to reflect the fact that over 70 per cent of mothers in our sample did not work at all at this stage in their children's lives. A statistical association between two variables can only be identified if both show sufficient variation – which was not the case for mothers' employment before their children's first birthday.

13 Other variables included in the regressions performed with MS and RS are: gender, cohort, seven age dummies, dummies for firstborn and only child, ever lived in a single-parent family by developmental stage, ever lived in a stepfamily by developmental stage, number of brothers and sisters, age of mother at child's birth (two dummy variables), age of father at birth (two dummy variables), mother's education (five dummy variables), father's education (five dummy variables), mother's and father's Hope-Goldthorpe measures of occupational prestige averaged over entire childhood, dummy variables for missing father and missing father's work history information, father's working time by developmental stage. Other variables included in the regressions performed with SMS and SRS are the sibling differences in: age, gender, firstborn, ever lived in a single-parent

family by developmental stage, ever lived in a stepfamily by developmental stage, mother's age at birth was 21 or less, mother's age at birth was 35 or more, father's age at birth was 21 or less, father's age at birth was 37 or more, mother's and father's Hope-Goldthorpe measures of occupational prestige averaged over entire childhood, missing father and missing father's history. A constant term is also included because of non-random sorting of siblings (Ashenfetter and Rouse,1999).

14 In their study of the 1970 birth cohort, Joshi and Verropoulou (2000) found that children whose mother was employed sometime while they were aged under five achieved significantly lower qualifications by the age of 26 than those whose mothers were not employed. When we adopted the same pre-school employment indicator variable with our data and used a between family estimator comparable to theirs, we obtained almost exactly the same result.

15 Full information on the results for each of the estimators and samples for the other outcomes can be obtained from the authors. [Found in the web-site annexe to this report www.iser.essex.ac.uk/jrf/ermij/annex.php]

16 The age effects detected with sibling differences, which combine age and cohort effects, were usually not statistically different from zero. The only exception was for economic inactivity, where being one year older significantly increased the probability of being inactive (by 1.3 per cent according to the restricted sample, SRS).

17 See tables in web-site annex.

18 See tables in web-site annex.

19 See tables in web-site annex.

20 They were able to estimate these effects more precisely because they used a larger sample of siblings, covering more birth cohorts.

21 While our preferred *sibling difference estimates* of the effects of parents' employment do not provide evidence on these favourable effects (because higher longer-term family income is common to siblings), the positive effects of the Hope-Goldthorpe score on educational attainment in the *between family estimates* are consistent with such favourable effects.